Strange, but UNIQUE!

I0154040

24 Felonies & 24 Alias'

A True Story

Justice Jones

Strange, but UNIQUE!

Published by Fountain of Life Publisher's House

P. O. Box 922612 Norcross, GA 30010
Phone: 404-936-3989
Please Email Manuscripts to: publish@pariceparker.biz
For all book orders including wholesale email:
sales@pariceparker.biz
To request author email: author@pariceparker.biz
www.pariceparker.biz

Fountain of Life Publishing House is committed to excellence in the publishing industry. The Company reflects the philosophy established by the founder, based on Psalm 68:11, *"The Lord gave the word and great was the company of those who published it."*

Book design copyright © 2016 by Parice C Parker. All rights reserved.
Cover Design by Parice C. Parker
Interior design by Parice C. Parker

Published in the United States of America

ISBN: 978-0692641828
02.10.2016

FORWARD

I have heard many stories and met countless individuals from all walks of life. However, this author is indeed *strange, but unique.* This book has touched deeply in many areas that most will shun away from, overlook and never have to encounter such things as this author has. Her story will make you more aware of terrible things that people experience and how quickly life could take a twist for the wrong turn. 24 Felonies & 24 Alias' made me see an author and not the criminal. One day as we were sharing the details of this book, Ms. Justice Jones said, "The system made me look like I'm a career criminal." And, 1 looked and thought. All these years and she were an author before she formed in her mother's womb. 24 Felonies & 24 Alias' is a TERRIFIC Book that will ignite your suspense, and it's *strange, but unique!*

Apostle, Parice C. Parker

Strange, but UNIQUE!

TABLE OF CONTENTS

Justice Jones

My Dedication

My life story is strange but unique. I have written the book and dedicated it to the work of the Lord. It's not about fine clothes and money for me but for lives to be encouraged and change for the good. I want to take this beautiful and blessed land back from the devil and help God's people. If we begin to come together, this vision can happen. Let us tear down these trap hotels and use them for shelters to help the homeless. Help bring them into the Kingdom of God by showing them love. His children are perishing for lack of knowledge. Let's bring the lost sheep in because we have the power to change some- body's world. God's elect is out here living in bondage. I know because I have been there. I had to live this life to tell this story. I just want people to stop, look, and listen to what the

Spirit of the Lord has for this land flowing in milk and honey.

I like to dedicate and thank every angel that God had camped around me through this journey here on earth. First and foremost, I dedicate my life story to my loving mother, the late *Helen Marie Jones.*

To my loving daughters that had to live this journey with me. I want to thank you for your love, and tough love. And thank you for never leaving me, I couldn't have made it without their love and prayers, and my four fabulous grandchildren. To all my sisters, and brothers who loved me in the mist of the storm.

The Work of the Lord

INTRODUCTION

It's easy to judge a book by the cover, but this is one book you must read thoroughly to get a full understanding. Justice Jones lived the life from the deck of cards that was dealt. So, she had to learn how to play the game of life the way she knew to survive. Nevertheless, she lived through hardcore struggles, was forced to be motherless at a very young age, and trained to survive by being pushed, and shoved to a life of chaotic crime. 24 Felonies & 24 Alias' is strange, but unique. Explore all Justice Jones had to endure after all she encountered, and a life she was forced to live!

Justice Jones

Vision

During one of my incarcerations in the D. C. Jail System, a woman came in my cell. She had a glow, and it was bright. I received this vision about 25 years ago. I was sitting on my bunk, and I was on the top. She walked over to me, and said, "Get down you have blood issues." I looked at her, and I was amazed. I couldn't move! I asked her, "What do you want, and why you here in jail telling me about blood issues." She answered her father was sick, and she cashed his check, but the bank had her locked up. Before I knew it, I climbed down from the bunk, and it was early in the morning. She told me, "Go to the water fountain, and bless the water then drink it," I did. And, by that time the officer called me to do my station, and the nurse wanted to know if anyone ever told me that I had a liver disorder? An inmate walked in right afterwards telling me that I have a blood issue, and at the same time the officer called me into the CO Station with the nurse on the phone. So, I go back to talk with the inmate, and she said, "Drink the water God is going to heal you." So I drank some more of the water, and I started to bleed from my uterus. She said, "Let's pray." As we were praying, she also said, "God wants you to read the book of Daniel." And, I did.

God showed me in a vision that I would write this book (24 Felonies and 24 Alias'), and He also showed me that I would be in The Lords Army. Now, I'm telling you all of my life story throughout this book God had me to envision years ago. I would have perished if God had not given me this vision. As you read some of my life story in 24 Felonies & 24 Alias', you will see that I had to go through what I went through to become who God predestined me to be. All of these years I was born to be an author, thank you, Jesus, for covering me through it all.

The Battle is Not Mine It Is the Lord's

Chapter 1

I want all readers of my testimony and life story on this earth to be an inspiration, although it's strange, it is unique. It took 24 Felonies along with 24 aliases to know that I was where God sent me at all times. When I went into the store, God went with me. I had no control over my life. Satan and God had a battle over me. I want you all to know, "Even the righteousness of God through faith in Jesus Christ to all, and on all who believe. There is no difference between you and me; for, we all have sinned and have fallen short of the Glory of God. Therefore, I am going to reveal to you, my life story. It was Jesus Christ, who has called me out of disobedience, in the spirit, and it will take place in the natural. So, that there is no condemnation because I no longer walk in the flesh. I have a life in the spirit from this day forward. Now, He commanded for no one to touch my anointed angel nor my prophet to be harmed. I tell the readers that we know that all things work together for the good of the Lord to those who truly love the Lord, and are called according to His purpose.

For God knew me before I knew myself and the will of my destiny. He had predestined me, and conformed me in the image of His son, Jesus Christ, and The Great I am? God predestined, and glorified me. Who can be against me? Remember, God did not spare His son, but delivered Him for all of us. So, therefore, thus said the Lord, who shall bring change against God's elected?"

It is God who justifies, and it is He who condemns! Only Christ died and sat at the right side. He makes intercessions for me. No one can separate me from Christ. Wherever I am, He will also be. No tribulation, no distress or persecution, perilous times or sword shall separate me from Christ. Be of the same mind toward one another, and be not wise in your opinion. Before, and now, I am more than a conquer in Jesus Christ.

Many days I felt a war going on inside me. One was God, and the other was Satan. Satan tried hard to convince me to do bad, but God always protected me in the mist of the situations. All of my life I felt unloved, had low self-esteem and felt like I was the black sheep of the family. Also, sometimes bearing all the weight, and stressing myself out allowing more baggage to weigh me down. I don't make excuses for my life, but many don't know what challenges I had to face every day. I was raised in harsh conditions, and I had to fight every day to survive. It's easy to go to school and get your education when you don't have to face hunger, homelessness, and poverty every day. Some people are more fortunate than others, and some have to endure greater life challenges to be the voice of others living in cruel conditions. You will see some of what I endured, and mine started at a very young age. I didn't even have a chance for a normal childhood, and to live an ordinary life. I often wonder how things would have been if the tragedy did not occur.

Center of the World Warren Ohio

Chapter 2

One day, in a town called Warren Ohio, a child of God was conceived in the year of 1954. I was born to Helen and Albert Jones in the year of 1955. My mother had nine children at the age of thirty, and I was second to the oldest.

Yes, a little bossy. I just wanted to do good by my family. I loved my mother, and always dreamed of buying mother a cute house. There were nine of us from the will of God for mom to give birth. I know many ridiculed my mother for bearing as many as she did, but I could not imagine my life without my siblings. We have had some hard times, but we all made it. My mother was an honest lady and loved her children. My mom loved all of us, and did the best she could to provide, but she also had a sin. It had a firm hold on her. That sin was men. She loved to be loved, therefore, her destiny in Christ, Jesus was to give birth to these nine children. One just happened to be me. Her love for men brought lots of pain, and sin for all the rigorous trials, and problems she had to endure at such a young age. One father to the next gave mom false hope and false dreams. I believe mother just wanted to live an ordinary life, happily married with the white picket fence, and to have a loving husband.

My mother used to get off work, and she would go out and help the teachers at school. She just loved children. As I was reminiscing one day, mother walked out of the store with a newspaper under her arms and forgot to pay for it. It was a hot summer day, and she made me run all the way back to pay for it. Man, was I mad. Mother was not a thief, I was. She was an honest woman about 5 ft. 5 in tall. Mother had a beautiful smile, pearly white teeth, jet black hair and she was big boned. I remember mother was allergic to sugar and whoever was bad their punishment was to scratch her back. Mom tried all she could to make our home happy and fitting. She's the best mother one could wish for.

I remember my stepdad used to bring home bags of fruit from the sanitation truck. Mom and my step dad had a lot of mouths to feed. He also, brought us our first color TV. He did some good things for the family, but I used to hate when he pulled that gun on Mother. I hated him for doing that. Times he grew angry he would wave his gun at her, and I always knew he was going to kill my mother one day. I felt it deep in my gut. My father was a man that sinned and brought trouble into her life, which caused a tragic death. February 14, 1970, was a day of much sorrow because my stepfather shot my mother. My mother wouldn't hurt a fly, sweet as she could be and harmless.

As I tell you all my story about my life, you will see a pattern of major disturbances. In everyone's life, they have patterns which lead to many different roads to turn. I was born under the common sign of Mercury. The planet, Mercury has a lot of movement, and it is very quick and so was I. As we explore the story of my life. Watch the signs! Watch and you'll see the pattern, a perfect pattern of the maze that God had traveled with me. When I was five years old, my life took a turn. I became a thief.

My father had the same sin. He was quick. He did things that sent him to prison. My mother struggled, and she was just a mother doing what moms do.

I went to an elementary school, and my teacher loved me. I was a lovable little girl but at the same time, full of mischief. I always wanted to be loved. One day, my second-grade teacher chose me to go on a shopping trip with two other kids. One of the other children was sick in the hospital. My family was poor. I wanted some money from my mother and father to go with the teacher, and so that I could have spending money. They said they did not have any. I wanted it so bad, I went into my mother's purse, saw one dollar, and made a decision. Well, I took the dollar, went to school, l and went shopping with the teacher. I bought myself a coloring book and crayons. I went home happy! When I got there, my father was waiting for me. He asked me, "Where did you get money to buy the coloring book and crayons?" Well, I lied. I told him that I got it from my teacher. He took my coloring book and crayons. He gave them to the other children, and he beat me. I was seven years old. Seven is the number of spiritual completion, so stealing had taken root in my flesh. When I was also a little girl in school, I would go to the community center. I would watch over a girlfriend from the other side of town. I wouldn't let anyone bother her. I lived on the west side, and she lived on the east side. She was my only friend. And, I loved her mother. The director of the community center loved me also. She knew my mother had lots of children plus lots of problems. She felt for these children, but I was special to her.

One day, this old lady's change purse was open, and the change got missing. She knew I was in there, and no other children had been in there that day. She would put her purse in the same spot every day for me to get change. Now, this lady had to be one of my angels because as I grew up and went to beauty school, this lady returned into my life. I had been to prison and back when I had seen this lady again. At beauty school, she would come onto the clinic floor. She did not want anyone to do her hair, but me. She loved me. If I were not on the floor that day, she would come back the next day. Her name was Ms. Arnold, and she was 60 years old. I loved Ms. Arnold. I also wish Ms. Arnold could read my life story. Thank you, God, for Ms. Arnold.

Now, we come to the part of my life that will take a ride down memory lane. My mother was a gentle lady, but my father was very mean, and unfaithful. He had a girlfriend who I'll always remember. That lady was mean and evil. She would follow my mother to the store, and try to fight her because she was going with my father. I hated that lady. I remember one day, my mom was coming from the store. We were outside. My mom was walking real fast. The lady was trying to catch her to fight my mom for her husband, but I was outside. I jumped in front of the lady and had a meltdown. My eyes turned red. The devil told me to kill her, but my mother made my other sisters and me, and brothers go to the house, and she locked the door. Right after that, my father went to prison for stealing appliances for this lady. He was the lookout. He went to sleep. They sent him to prison. On his way to prison, he had a soul friend who I called a so-called-friend. He asked him to take care of my mother, and his eight children at the time. He asked him to look out for her. Now my life was sad, and miserable at such a tender age. I felt that my mother loved my oldest sister more than me. I can remember that my oldest sister was so pretty. She got beautiful clothes, with all sorts of colors; light pink, yellow, orange, etc. I got clothes that weren't pretty to me like blue, brown, purple, and red. They were real dark colored. I always felt like she got more attention than I did, but nevertheless, I didn't know then, what I know now. I had more attention than one could ever hope. Well, remember, life is a pattern of what you make it in your mind. So, therefore, I paid a lot of attention to my oldest sister. She had lots of boyfriends, and I didn't. I would act like a tomboy. I beat them up.

Well, my early teenage years went on, and I had lots of fights in school with girls. They made fun of my shape. My oldest sister had a lovely shape. I grew up with low self-esteem, and I had problems with myself. Being young with really no guidance, you take on the environment. I already hated myself. I remember that my mother had gotten a new boyfriend, and he came to live with us. I didn't like him at all. He was controlling, and he used to be mean to my mother. I would ramble about their things. I was very inquisitive, and I would steal his money out of his wallet when he wasn't around. I didn't want his money because I would just go to school and buy my so-called-friend lunch. I didn't want it for me. Also, one day, I was rambling, and looked under the mattress, and found a drug needle. I knew that he acted funny and angry, but I didn't realize that he was on drugs! I didn't like him then.

My mother was naive and she probably never knew. Since I was the unfortunate little child, who got a whooping all the time. I would never be anybody. So, they thought that I wasn't going to be anybody. He had a Christian sister with lots of children, so they had her to take me to church. I never forgot this church. One Sunday, we were in church, and the preacher said, "It's someone out there that has a word for the church." I got up and moved to the front of the church, and this is what happened. I walked to the front of the church then I begin to sing a song, and this is how it went:

You can't beat God's Giving, No matter how hard You try, the more, You give the more, He gives to you, So keep on giving, Cause I know, it's really true God was preparing me for the future. As we go further into my life story, I remember the patterns in my life. God sets patterns in your life, and the flesh and evil spirits set patterns in your life too. Now, it comes to a tragic tale that carried me to another part of this maze called the wilderness (Egypt). I went to high school at the age of fourteen. I was in the 9th grade, and something happened. I used to go downtown, get off the bus to transfer to another and go home but between getting on the next bus, I would go shoplifting. The pattern of stealing began at a very early age in my life. I just could not help myself. I felt like I was purposed to steal.

Pre – Meditated Murder, Man - Slaughter or Homicide?

Chapter 3

I would tip toe in the room while my mother and stepfather were asleep, and take what I could out of his pockets. The next day I would buy something. I had money because I used to steal from my mother's boyfriend. Stealing was always in me even from early childhood. Besides, I didn't like him because he would always threaten mom with his gun. I used to hate for him to come home because he loved putting fear in my mom. Some days he made her laugh and smile then others she cried. I never could understand why he fussed at mom because she was always trying to do her best to please him. Mom only wanted to be happy. This is the man my father gave permission to take care of his wife, and kids while he went to prison, but dad didn't realize all the trauma this man was going to put his family through. Many days mom and I feared for our life, but time kept moving forward, and tension in our home grew worst.

So I stepped up to the plate to try, and make mom happy, and not realizing my habit of shoplifting grew stronger and stronger. Life matters where and how a child is raised. I used to feel alone, ugly, unloved, and at times, I became desperate and needed to feel a void. I never knew how it felt to have a loving dad taking care of his children, and a happy mom living under the same roof. I always wondered what it would be like if things would have been different? Oh well, that's life I guess and I have to live mine. If mom only knew, and many days I believe she wanted the same thing I wanted. Somebody got to make mom happy – it's about to be Christmas. I would get a bag, and steal household goods, and whatever I could get away with when I was shoplifting. Often, I used to run away from this policewoman, and she would always watch me. She knew that I was stealing, but she could never keep up with me on foot. I loved what I did, at least, that's what I thought. It gave me a feeling of acceptance because what I was taking was not for me. It was for my mother, sisters, and brothers. We were so poor we couldn't afford nice things. So, I would shoplift because I didn't have the money to get my family nice stuff. I wanted so badly to take care of my family and to make mom happy. I used to love to see her smile. I would wrap up all of my gifts that I had stolen, and take them home. It was Christmas time. My mother would ask me where did I get the money. I told her that I had a job at the local jewelry store as a wrapper. I would put all of my gifts in the closet, until we got our Christmas tree. This was the only Christmas that I remembered before that tragic day. Christmas came, and my mother, sister, and brothers opened their gifts from me. I didn't get many, but it's didn't matter because I gave a lot in making my family smile. I only had what mom bought me, but nevertheless, my mother had her last Christmas, and her very best Christmas. She had gotten things that she never had because I stole them for her. My mom deserves the world, and I loved my mom. My mother had sheets, dishes, small appliances, jewelry, clothes, etc. They didn't come from thrift stores either. I wanted mom to have the best. They were not hand me downs because that's all I could remember and the saddest thing about it was there were never gifts for my mom before then.

We used to get one big gift. On that Christmas, we had gotten a bumper pool table. "Do you remember the table with the studs in the middle?" We also had gotten one of those shields to put in front of the black and white T. V. to make them colored. That's how poor we were. Mom was so happy that Christmas she remembered it as one of the most beautiful Christmases she'd ever had.

Feb. 3rd. My sister and I were in the bedroom playing pool. The pretty one. My step-father came in. He was helping her to shoot pool. He was standing behind her and hovering over her. I saw him take his hands out of her blouse feeling on her breast. He didn't know I saw him. He was making a pass at my sister. So, I left out the bedroom and went to tell mom. I went into the kitchen and told my mother about this man. Then, I went, and told my sister; I just told mother about trying to mess with you. By that time, I heard an argument, and I heard him tell my mom he was going to beat me, by that time he walked in the living room. I heard him call me with a loud voice, "Justice, Justice!" He had his belt in his hand and kept shouting louder and louder, "Justice!, Justice!" I ran outside, and he came. He and my mom ran behind me. She knew he was going to try and beat me, so she was attempting to get to me before he did. I heard mom calling, "Justice!" I stopped because my mom called me. I looked at my mother, and I told her, he Is going to kill you. So, I ran, and I ran until I got to grandmother's house. He was furious that I told my mom about him trying to mess with my sister as I had done something wrong. I wasn't going to stay around, and get a whooping for something I didn't do wrong. All the time I was running I was praying that Grandmother or someone would be at her house. I was tired, crying, and thirsty. I finally made it to my grandmother's house. Whew, that was the longest time it took me to get to grandmother's house. The more I ran the farther grandma's house seemed to be. I didn't have a good feeling about my mother.

Monday Never Came

Chapter 4

On February 15th, which was 12 days after I told her that she would be killed. He shot her! Now, my mother had gone out on Valentine's Day, February 14th with my auntie. And they ran into my real father that had gotten out of prison. Mom was talking to my real father, and my stepfather walked in. He was jealous and slapped my mother. So my aunt brought my mom home. Mom came home and prepared herself for bed. Soon afterward, my step-father came home in a rage. He was terribly mad at mom. He pulled his car around to the back door and barricaded it in. He didn't want mom to have a backdoor exit. My mom let him in, trying to calm him down, and they begin arguing. Oh, my God, he is mad, fussing and cursing mom out. Our next door neighbor saw the car at the back door and heard them arguing. So, she called the police.

The police arrived, and they instructed her to come to the police station on Monday morning to file charges. And, they told him to leave the house and left. So mom went upstairs and got into the bed with my sisters. No, if the police would have arrested him for abusing mom then, he would have been in jail, and mom would still be alive. Early that morning around 6 AM. He knocked on the door, BAM, BAM, BAM! Mom ran downstairs to answer the door. When she opened the door, he came in drunk. He started fussing, and cursing at her, again. He was loud, and tension was roaring. This is why I say it was Pre-Meditated murder. He had time to think about what he was going to do to mom, and how he was going to kill her. If the police would have arrested him. Perhaps, he would have cooled off or wouldn't have made bond. It was his second time at the door, and she didn't want her children to hear them arguing. She went back to the bedroom and closed the door. I knew mom was always afraid of him, and she didn't want us to see him abuse her. So, many days she thought she was hiding the abuse, but we heard it, over and over. After five or ten minutes, they heard a gunshot, POW! My siblings heard a gunshot! Oh My GOD! All of the children ran to see what had happened. All they heard him say was, "It was an accident!" He didn't mean to shoot her. My mother is laying there bleeding to death! He was ranting with tears in his eyes as if he was the victim and mom trying to hang in the balance fighting for her life.

See, this is what makes me angry. The days that I got caught shoplifting, and immediately I was arrested. The justice system protects the store merchandise before they protect someone's kids from losing their mother. The store owner gets 72 hours to file the warrant on the shoplifter. Why, can't it be the same for domestic violence? Isn't life more valuable than merchandise? Only, if they would have arrested my stepfather? He would have been incarcerated instead of making foolish plans to murder my mom. My stepfather should have gone to jail the first time the police came out.

Monday never came for mom. Remember; the police told her to come and file a warrant for his arrest. Nevertheless, Monday never came for mom. I was at my grandmother's house because the evil one's plan was to kill me! I felt it in my spirit and tried to warn mother the day I ran away to grandmother's house. Also, He was Satan! He knew what God had in store for me. Satan knew that I would be the one who would take over my mother's life here on earth to carry on, and write this story. I have lived with this for over 45 years. On the morning of February 15th, I was getting ready for school or something. It was a lovely sun shining day. I was up, and my grandmother's phone rang. I answered it. It was my oldest sister again. She said, "Nelson done shot mommy!" I said, "Is she dead?" My sister replied, "I don't know, she can't move." I dropped the phone, and I ran all the way to my mother's house. When I got there, mom was taken to the hospital, and the police were taking him to jail. My mom was in the Intensive Care Unit, and we would only see her on the hour for five minutes. The police came to the hospital, and my mother was unable to speak. They told her to put an X for her name because it was an accident. She told my grandmother that she did it because she didn't want him to hurt any of her children. Even on the hospital bed near death mom was afraid of him. He was cruel and vicious to my mom. I told mom he was going to kill her, and when she previously called the police, they should have arrested him. Look at all this could have been avoided, and my mother would have never made the front page of the Warren Tribune, "Mother of Nine Dies." It should have been Mother of Nine Murdered! And, remember it was nine of us that could never hear our mother's laughter again, get her loving support and parenting advice. We were all so young, and would live the rest of our lives without our mother. Monday, Warren Police Department ruled the death of my mom. Monday never came for her. I was only

13 years old, and I was second to the oldest. There was nothing we could do, but to call on God!

This is an article from Warren Tribute Newspaper that I am sharing. It was published in February 1970 about my mother's shooting.

This is Article 1 on February 17ᵗʰ, 1970

May Charge Man Today:
Mother of 9 Dies; Homicide Is Ruled

Charges were expected to be filed today by city police against a year – old Warren man in connection with the shooting death of a mother of nine here.

Mrs. Helen Jones, 30, 253 Lane SW, died at 6:45 p. m., Monday at Trumbull Memorial Hospital with a bullet wound to the neck sustained Sunday morning at home.

Trumbull Coroner Dr. Joseph Sudimack has ruled her death a homicide, the County's fourth homicide of the year and a city second.

According to the police, the suspect and Mrs. Jones were arguing in her home and a 25 caliber gun the man had in his right hand discharged during a struggle.

Police took the suspect into custody at the home and covered the weapon.

I know it was Pre – Meditated Murder. If the police would have done their job, and taken him to jail the first time, then my mother would still be living today. The criminal justice is all mixed up, and people like me are forced to live a different life because all children need the contribution of their parents love. Parents are the only security blanket a child have, and my mother was taken.

This is Article 1 on February 18th, 1970

Man Is Bound Over In Shooting Death

Nelson Clark, 34, of Warren, was bound to the Trumbull grand jury on a charge of first degree manslaughter after pleading innocent Tuesday in Warren Municipal Court. He waved his preliminary hearing and was released after posting a $3,000 bond. Mother of Nine -

Clark was charged with the shooting death of Mrs. Albert (Helen Beaver) Jones, 30, 253 Lane SW. A mother of nine, Mrs. Jones was shot once in the neck during an argument at her home Sunday morning and died Monday night at Trumbull Memorial Hospital.

Police took Clark into custody at the scene shortly after the shooting and confiscated a 25 caliber weapon. Trumbull Coroner Dr. Joseph Sudimack Jr. ruled the death a homicide.

Funeral services for Mrs. Helen will be held Thursday at 1 p. m. in Eastside Church of Christ. Friends may call at the Ross Funeral home from 7 – 8 p. m. Today.

Born here April 18th , 1939 she was the daughter of Ethel Crout Beaver and the late Robert J. Beaver.

She was a member of Eastside Church of Christ.

She was a graduate of West Junior High School, and was an instructor in the head start program in First Street School last summer.

Besides hey mother of Warren, she leaves her husband, Albert Jones, whom she married September 22, 1956; seven daughters, Sherrie L., Diane, Theresa, Carolyn, Felicia, Vannessa and Kimberly, two sons Albert and Jake, all of Warren; eight brothers, Robert H., Beaver of Geneva, N.Y, Alferd, Fred, John, Richard, Roosevelt,

Douglas, and Donald Beaver; and two sisters. Beatrice Kirksey and Mrs. Mary Lemon, both of Warren.

No Mo Mom – Blind Justice

Chapter 5

On the 15th, they took my oldest sister to see my mom for the last time. They skipped over me and took the rest of the children on the hour. They made sure that they took my brother who is under me, and then they took each, one by age. I was taken to see her last. Well, I thank God, because I got her last words. She said, "Justice, I know they say you are my bad child. Please don't let them split up my children," and then she went to sleep, that is what I thought. By the time I got to my mother's house, my grandmother was on the phone, and I knew, mom was gone. I believe she took her last breath as I was leaving. And, if I only would have known that would be my last time to see mom I would have hugged, and kissed her. Then, it was time to go, and view her body for his last time. My grandmother was shocked, and a tear wouldn't fall. She was startled! Those days went fast. We were at the home going service, and I sat next to my father. He was crying like a newborn baby. I just looked at him because he was the number one reason for her death. He gave the killer permission to take care of his family. He was the one that told the killer, "Man can you take care of my wife, and children while I do time for a crime." The kids and my daddy were all crying; my sister and brothers were crying too. My oldest sister was all over the casket. I just looked at what was going on around me. I didn't know at the time why I wasn't crying. I put spit on my eyes because I didn't want anybody to think I did not care. I just could not cry. God had given me peace with what happened. The kind of peace that passes all understanding. He had called me into the justice system, and my life began as mother's ended. From the ages of 15 to 20, I struggled to do what my mother's last words and wish was. Now, my oldest sister was with child at the home going. She was about 14 years old. She had her first child, but she didn't fall into my mother's footsteps. I did. My life story unfolds in this book. Remember, if you live by the sword, you die by it. What so ever you sow, that you shall reap, and I do mean every one of us, and everything. Now, and forever. I'll go on with my story since it was mom's end and my beginning.

Expedited Charges

Chapter 6

On February 17, 1970, this is what was in the headlines for my mother on the front page.

May Charge Man Today
Mother of 9 Dies
Homicide is ruled

Charges were expedited to be filed today by the city police against a 34-year-old Warren man in connection with the shooting death of a mother of 9 here. Mrs. Helen Jones, 30, died at 6:45 pm, Monday at Trumbull Memorial Hospital with a bullet wound to the neck sustained on Sunday morning at her home.

"Did you notice how the Trumbull Coroner, Dr. Joseph Sudimack had ruled her death a homicide?" It was the county's fourth homicide of the year and the city's second. According to the police, the suspect and Mrs. Jones were arguing in her home and a 25 caliber gun, the man had in his hand discharged during a struggle. Police took the suspect into custody at the home and recovered the weapon.

49

The coroner ruled homicide and the police ruled it an accidental death. "Somebody tell me how did that work?" I'm going to show you all when God called me in the Blind Justice." On the next day, he had a bond *Man Bound Over In Shooting Death*

Nelson Clark, 34 of Warren was bound to the Trumbull grand jury on a charge of first-degree manslaughter after pleading innocent Tuesday in Warren Municipal Court. He waived his preliminary hearing and was released after posting a $3,000.00 bond. Clark was charged with the shooting death of Helen Jones, 30 years old, a mother of 9. Mrs. Jones was shot once in the neck during an argument at her home on Sunday morning, and died Monday night at T. M. Hospital. This information is according to the newspaper.

Dr. Joseph Sudimock ruled her death a homicide. Now, that was the first case that God had given to me in the justice system. That became my calling.

Now, remember, my name is Justice Jones, called by God before I formed in my mother's womb. Let's look back at the first courtroom that involved my mother's death. Keep open mind readers. I have a case to look at. At the age of fourteen when that happened. I could not understand how that man, charged with homicide on the first day of the crime. And, on the second day of the crime manslaughter police charged him against the coroner rule. I called that Blind Justice. He killed her! The first time they told her that they couldn't take him to jail, and that she had to come down on Monday to file a warrant must have crushed the little bit of spirit that was left in her. Well, they made him leave her house, and there were 8 children in her home that night. To what avail, he came back at 6:45 am on that Sunday morning and killed her! I pleaded with the thoughts in my head to please help me to understand back when I was just 14! I wondered, "What is the justice system?" After that incident, there was no justice system or justice in our police department. After 60 years of pain and sorrow, I'm finally sharing my story with the United States of America.

I will tell you that God chose me before the foundation of this world to carry out his will for my life. I prevailed. When God takes charge, and that's just what he did for Mrs. Helen Jones.

One night, I was at a club, and I was 15. When I walked in, a man walked up to me, and said, "Nelson Clark just left here in a body bag." His girlfriend that he was going with behind my mother's back had just shot, and killed him dead.

God saw fit to bring him back to get His JUSTICE. For that, I said, "When God is for you; what can be against you?" My mother, and her 9 children saw justice by the Almighty God within one year. I knew that I did not have any harsh feelings when I saw him on that tragic day. I knew in my heart, spirit and my flesh that he was going to pay. You reap what you sow. God is the same yesterday, today, and tomorrow. Let no one think that you will get away from anything including myself. When I was shoplifting, I was punished.

As I go on with my story you will see the pattern. Now, it's time for me to carry on. My mother's work was done on this earth. I feel she was robbed of her life because our mother was taken from us, and gone too soon. My father was with his other girlfriend, and family. My mother's nine children stayed with grandmother in the same house that my mom was killed in. My father never came to take care of his kids. He was the one who ordered this man to be the man he should have been. And gave permission to take care of his family. I was only 14 years old. I had to ask myself, "Where were the men of God?"

Looking for Love in All The Wrong Places

Chapter 7

When I returned to school, I was bitter. I didn't want to be there. I started picking with a little girl in the bathroom. She made a comment that went through my heart. She was a white girl. She called me out of my name and then talked about my mother. I beat her good and got kicked out of school. I was sent to night school. That ended my schooling until later in life.

I saw my grandmother sell her property down to the last dime, and lived out of her suitcase when she lived with us. The benefits she received for nine children still left us with little means of survival. We were poor, and my grandmother struggled to take care of us. At that time, my grandmother had to take care of 9 children with her social security check. Yes, we were very, very poor. Mother did not take out insurance, so all 7 of her brothers and sisters had to pay for her funeral arrangements. We had nothing. I remember my sisters, and brother had to struggle so hard. "No way," I said.

At the age of 17, I was abused by a man 16 years older than me. He had four children of his own, but I was looking for love in the wrong places. At the age of 18, I had a baby girl. This baby girl was the beginning of motherhood. I had six sisters, and two brothers, and a child. This older man forced himself on me. One day he took me to the woods and forced me to be with him. He screwed me, and a baby was born. Eventually, I fell in love with this man, but I thank God for this man regardless even when he shot me because I have a child. And, that alone is priceless to me. She ended up being one of my angels when I was out in the wilderness. Now, I'm going into motherhood, and I need a job, and I needed to keep my freedom.

I went to a job interview at the steel mill in our hometown called Lordstown. They made parts for General Motors. My baby girl was five days old. I didn't want to leave her, and I knew that if I kept stealing, I was going to jail one day. Well, Lordstown called me with a job. I was happy, and ready to go to work, and help grandmother, so I went on the job interview to take the physical. Now, the word was that you couldn't be overweight, and I had just had a baby. The doctor who took my physical was real fat. The people who I saw in line were fat, so I was scared because I needed the job. When the nurse took my weight, I changed it on the paper, and I think that the doctor had noticed. He told me, "You passed the physical, all but one part." He said, "You are 30lbs. Overweight and if you want this job, I will tell you what to do." He said, "You need to lose one pound a day for thirty days, and you can begin to work on the 31st day." I tell you, he must have been 400lbs. I looked at him and said, "How am I supposed to do that?" He said, "Don't eat nothing that comes from under the ground like potatoes, carrots, and things that come from under the earth." I looked at him, and said, "You lose 30lbs!" I didn't have time to wait. I had sisters, and brothers that were hungry, and needed to eat. We were penniless and didn't have no money. I was desperate I had a job to do, and no time to waste. Whatever it took I had to do.

I quit night school. I used to leave every morning like I was still in school. I used to watch the drug addicts. At that time, they were drinking, smoking, shooting heroin, etc… I didn't like people who got high in school. I thought that I was too good to do those things. Soon after, I hung out with some heroin addicts because they were always high, and always had money. There was this one guy who always sold merchandise, and I asked him one day, could I go shoplifting with you. That was when my shoplifting career took off, and my prison life began. I was busy, and at the same time, it was working out. At least, I thought it was. Remember, you reap what you sow. I was stealing, and I knew that I would go to jail one day.

I would go shoplifting with this guy, and for about three years then I got caught for stealing, they put me on probation. Life had dealt me this hand. If you could ask me now if I would had done it any other way, I would have told you, "Yes." But, every door got closed in my face. We are not people of choice but of environment. If you have never been where I have been, you probably would not understand, but neither did I.

Lordstown turned me down. When we lived in a small town where that doctor knew about the mother of 9 killed, and that I was her child, he didn't care so neither did I. I wasn't going to be rejected once again, so I did what I thought I had to do. I didn't know then what I know now. I was still working out God's plan for me in the flesh. Remember readers, we all have sinned, and we all have a destiny. In our lives, God puts all of us here to do his will. As I go into the next chapter, you will see the pattern.

First Incarceration

Chapter 8

When I turned 21, my baby was three years old, and I was on my way to prison for shoplifting in Ohio. It was a reformatory for women. Now, I was sentenced in my hometown for no less than six months, and no more than five years. I was on probation when the judge sentenced me, and my daughter was with her auntie. Her father was absent in her life. You will hear me say, "Where were all the men?" again but nevertheless, life goes on.

While I was in prison, God was showing me what was coming. I read all of Donald Goines books and Ice Burge Slim books. These books were the life that I was heading for. They were about dope fiends, a black girl lost and hustlers. As I continue with my life story, you will see the patterns and my life how God had prepared me for my forty years' probation under God's watch. See, the prison was not prison to me. It was the home of the Lord to me. I was sick, and I was lost. So that he took me out of Egypt. It was the wilderness, the place where I was lost doing the things that I thought I had to do to survive. At that prison, it was a resting area for me. I remember, when I first got there, I would look out of the window, and watch the ladies walk around the dock, coming from lunch.

There was a girl there who I adored because she always had a smile on her face, and she was gay. That was the first time a gay person was of some interest to me. She sat out from the other women.

There, I did not know I was being introduced to that spirit. Just to let you all know, in the later part of my story, you will hear me speak of that spirit.

That girl had something else going on. She had on different clothing than most of the ladies there. Her clothes were unique. They were called honor uniforms, for people who lived in the honor dorms, and they called them prints. She had evil spirits and good spirits. I would run and look out the window to see her. I didn't know that God was teaching me something, so I tried to get to the dorm that she was in. We used to write notes because I was in admissions, and had to be there until we were classified for the population. As God was showing me the art of God behavior, setting goals to excel, and then the devil wanted to lure me in. That was my goal to get where she was. At that time, she was my inspiration to make it to her area in prison, because in her dorm area they received special privileges; such as stay up later, special visitations, etc.

I remember, I have always been an active lady. I had to be strong from the age of 14. Remember, I had to be about my father's business (God). I had to live out my mother's last words. See, in that prison, I had seen things that weren't right on the staff. I could not understand why I was in jail for my petty crimes when there were bigger crimes that happened right in front of me! They had a work detail that we made license plates for the state of OHIO. We also put traffic tickets into the computers or on records. People that they knew, they threw their traffic tickets away.

Those traffic tickets did not go on the records because there were no computers back then. I had seen where cops showed favoritism. I didn't understand. I asked myself again, "Why was I there in the midst of all those bad things?

One day, I was playing cards, and a girl bully approached me. And she tried to start a fight with me. My intentions was to keep her off of me. So I picked up the coffee pot, and it was boiling water! Satan wanted me to stay there for life, but God had another plan. The water burnt no one. It hit the floor instead. God delivered me out of his hands again! I didn't receive any disciplinary actions for it.

I could not go to the honor dorm if I were ever in trouble. I had done six months, and it came time to go and see the parole board. Ohio's parole board was different than Georgia's. From what I have experienced, you had to go in front of them in the flesh. There were six of them, and they would ask you questions. I remember them asking me that if I could live my life over, would I live it in the same way. I answered them, and this is what I said, "I would live it in the same way because I had a choice to make. After looking for a job and the door closed in my face when I knew that I could do the job, and so did they, I didn't have time for that. We had to eat, we had to put on clothes, and we had to survive. I'll do it the same way."

This is what they said to me, "We want to let you go home, but we can't." You were on probation so you must do six months for violating probation. We will see you again in 6 more months." After six months, they came back, and I had no DR's. I still lived in the honor dorm, and they released me back into Egypt to be about my Father's business (God's).

Life had dealt me a hand, and I had to play it. I know that some of my readers don't agree. No one knows what God has in store for you or me, but it's okay to disagree. For me to come home at that time was when my daughter's life began. I was back in Warren to be who I was going to become. He was there for me then, and He's there for me now.

Let me tell you about my life after being released from Marysville, Ohio. When I got out, everything was still the same. Grandmother had no help. The kids still had struggles, needed clothes, etc. So my shoplifting went on. I caught another case. God covered me, and I got out of it. It was time for me to exit Ohio. One day, I went into a department store and filled up a bag. When I walked out, the store's security officer caught me. I told them that a lady in the store had put items in the bag for me. I made it believable, and they let me go. At the time, God removed me from harm and I returned to Marysville Ohio.

Where Is Justice Second Chance?

Chapter 9

For years, I thought I was running the race in vain. It is a lovely thing when you have a vision. It is even better when you feel like you are not alone. I want to take you back to the last twenty years. I lost in more ways than one. I was lonely, hurt, and longing for the love of my mother for many days. I never asked for this life. I used to look how other families were normal, happy and celebrating holidays. I was robbed of the opportunity of coming home from school, and momma had dinner waiting and a surprise awaiting us. No one could feel the years of torture, trauma, and suffering I endured along with my siblings. I was calling out to God, and He was right there, but I had to get to understand

Him for myself. I know He loved me because I was in some crazy, and life threatening situations that many did not make it out alive. He went everywhere I went.

So when I left Ohio prison, I come home, and I had a different kind of respect for myself. I didn't think it was right to hustle. So God showed me favor, and I received a Scholarship to go to beauty school. I wanted to do what was right. I wanted to change, and I didn't want to lose my daughter being in and out of jail. I met this guy, John, and he was the guy all the girls were going crazy over, and all the girls wanted him. I knew of John from my old neighborhood, and he was a player. I got a job at a local department store called Strouss, and it was in a mall-like atmosphere. We worked in the beauty salon area after we had completed beauty school. I am headed in all the right directions cleaning my life up. It wasn't one week this store manager previously remembered me from one of his stores. He wanted me terminated immediately! He must have remembered me from shoplifting before. So, I asked my boss to let me speak to this store manager, and he said, "Why would I put cheese in the cage with a rat?" It tore me up inside. So another door was closed in my face. The company I worked for was inside his store, and they let me go. Nobody wanted to give me a second chance. So eventually, I got married to John hoping that would better my life. John was a good looking, slim and handsome guy, but it was awkward how we begin our relationship. I sought love in all the wrong places. Nevertheless, I finished beauty school. One day at beauty school this chick was looking at me wrongfully, cocking her eyes, and she was dating

John at the time. Since all the girls wanted him, I thought it would be the perfect timing to take him from her not knowing the devil comes behind bedroom eyes. I disliked John's girlfriend at the time because she was picking at the hump on my hips since they set up high. So I said, "You like to play it like that. I'm going to get your man tonight, and see how he like this hump." John was very fine. He was like a Mr. Good-bar, but I didn't like him to get serious. I was just going to sleep with him once to make her mad, and we continued a relationship afterward. Oh, we had some good, and bad moments. So many it would require me to write another book. I thought it was going to be one night because I knew John from an old neighborhood, and he was too much of a player. And, yes he had the past. One day I pulled up on John because I had a car, and she didn't. I was around 21 years old, and when he saw me, he also saw dollar signs. At the time, John was about 25. I remembered hearing rumors that he had gone to prison for killing somebody. And, this is the sort of thing I heard but I still gave him a second chance. His brother was a drug user, and messed up some drug money, but the drug dealer pistol-whooped his brother and left him in the woods to die. John and his other brother were angry, so they went and found the drug dealer with a sawed-off shot gun and shot up the hotel. All this had happened before I met John. Now, they killed the drug dealer that had brutally assaulted his brother, but the drug dealer was with a girl. She got shot as they were firing, and her wounds left her blind. This white girl ends up being the Judge's daughter they didn't kill her, but she was left shot, and blind. However, she was the one that identified them through their voices. I wonder if that was justice for real. How are you going to hear a voice through all the loud noise with the gun shots? If she hadn't recognized them through their voices, they would have gotten away. John's brother got life in prison for this crime, and John's mother begged him, don't do a jury trial please plead insanity. So John did and spent several years incarcerated. See, I knew of John from our previous neighbor, and I heard many rumors, but I stilled hooked up with John. I was acting like a witch and took her man then later I got married. See once we slept together I begin to shower him with love because I had big money at the time. Remember, I was a hustler and had to make a living. So I always had all the latest things, fashions, and the hottest items. OMG! Let me tell you how that happened. As we progressed in our relationship sooner than later I got married. I felt John was using me for a money machine. In the beginning of our relationship, I didn't mind, I just thought he loved me as I loved him but after time went by things begin to change. One day we went to my friend's wedding she was a white girl, and John loved to show off especially we being one of the few black people there. I told Kacey, my friend, "Make sure you throw me the bouquet." I caught it, and I couldn't believe it! John was a show off rascal, and he shouted we are getting married in 7 days. This man said, "You can't pull that off in 7 days," but John did. The man had a good job. John loved nice things and popularity. He thought the man was probably going to show up with big gifts, and money but he did not even come. John was a show-off, and a seven-day wedding was a great challenge for us. We planned, gathered, and had a wedding in 7 days. Sometimes, now I still laugh at how we pulled it off. We got married in November, and the next November we moved to Atlanta, Georgia. Finally, life seems to be looking good for me until that hot water was thrown directly towards my face.

Life Is Not Fair
Chapter 10

At times I missed my mother, and her death was unjustified. She got one bullet wound to the neck, and when her murderer was arrested, he got released on a $3,000.00 bail. What kind of justice system let a killer out for killing a mother of nine children and only have a $3,000.00 bond? My mom's death was cruel and unjustified! Nevertheless, I got caught shoplifting with two Easter dresses I and got a $50,000.00 bond. I never understood how this justice system works, when they protect the real criminals as if mom's life was nothing, and did not matter. I know many people criticize and talk about me, and some even said, "I'm crazy." But, God called me in into the justice system, and I went in on the inside. I believe I was His eyes, and His detective to gather evidence. So, I can tell my story. To also, bring awareness to how unfair our justice system is. How else would I have made it all this way if it had not been for the Lord on my side? So, many of us have different walks of life, and mine was strange but unique.

My shoplifting cover took off, life became a whirlwind, mom was gone, grandma came to be with us. Nine children, we had no welfare, no social security, just our uncle, and two aunts on my father's side. I like to take the time to thank my father's side of the family. I love you all; this is a personal story one of many to come. See, I was at a Jr. High School bitter, mean and evil, remember I was ugly, but I wasn't, but that's how people made me feel. They made fun of my shape, but I'm here to tell you, "I'm beautifully and wonderfully made."

The horse, the horse – the horse I have saddled up and it's time for me to run out in the wilderness one day shortly after my pass.

We saddled up and moved to Atlanta, Georgia. God gave me a vision before I left. Life will perish without a vision. In Revelations, there is a white horse, and that horse had a sword and a scale. It was a lady with blinds on. I couldn't get her out of my mind. I was that lady on my way to the Metro Atlanta. Not knowing the devil had stumbling blocks ahead, and he had a plan for me. I had a plan, and God had a plan for me too. As I go on with my story, you will see the pattern of the Blind Justice. So many ignore the signs of a disfigured life but through all my difficult times I was able to see, and hear what the voice of the Lord was telling me so I could show the world. Our Justice system is blind and corrupt.

Colony Farm was a prison, but it was a hospital to me. One day I was in church, and we sang Pass Me Not Oh Gentle Savior Do Not Pass Me By ... when I got to singing SAVIOUR I was screaming above the choir. I was thunderous, and I wanted JESUS to hear me singing. The Bishop came over to me after church, and she told me, "Jesus is not that far, He never left you." I was there about four months, and this was my first prison sentence in Georgia. You wouldn't believe all my eyes saw, the things I heard, and the things I experienced. I don't want to get into detail or cause harm to anyone. So, I'd rather just say the staff wasn't professional. There were rumors that the inmate used to leave the facility to do the lawns of the staff. A death row inmate escaped on a tractor, and a few got pregnant, but they had abortions. This was the rumors that were going on when I was there after a while. I finished my time. There was a lot going on there too at the halfway house, drugs, sex and drama. One day on the way back to the house I relapsed. Soon as I stepped through the doors, and they gave me a drug test. I didn't pass. I know it was only God. Again, He spared me and granted me favor. The lieutenant called me on the phone, and this is what she said, "I don't know who your God is but you need to get down on your hands, and knees and thank Him because I was on my way back to take you back to jail."

I finally got released back to the wilderness. I still had children, needed somewhere to stay and probation to pay. Now, my husband was not there when times got rough.

I had a shoplifting case for stealing my

children two Easter dresses, and they sent me to prison. At this time, my husband had been in and out of the mental hospital. As he had done something very, very, very bad and they gave him a floater to another state and told him if he comes back to the state of GA, he would have to serve 15 years. The justice sentence gave him a second chance; but, I got ten years, do two. And a $50,000.00 bond. God was there with me, and He lead me to a good lawyer, and my bond was reduced to $5,000.00. Now, was that justice?

Exit On Candler Rd

Chapter 11

My husband and I passed our exit and ended up on Candler Road. Immediately, I started looking for a real job, but couldn't find a job; that could take care of my family.

I came to the south, and all I hear is missing and murdered children. It was a reporter named Monica, and she was discussing something about children stolen out of their bedrooms. It was a lot of rumors, and on the news everywhere. Now I have a child of my own. What are they talking about? I know that God is going to reveal it, but I don't understand. And I thought in my mind maybe this is not the place I should be. Missing, and murdered children? We settled in our first apartment, and on the 3rd day, we had an ice-storm. I walked outside my house, and it had covered the whole Metro Atlanta area. I know this was a sign for me to remember. I just entered the justice system. It is time for me to experience, so now I am looking for a job, Glenwood, Memorial Drive, Candler Rd and I noticed there was a liquor store, beauty salon and on every corner. I begin to see all the stores, malls, and shopping centers. Remember, I am from a small town, and it looks like a big Christmas tree to me. I saw success everywhere. I found out about this program called CETA. I am ready to make a difference in my life. The Lord gave me a job at this big non – profit organization. It is still thriving today, and I don't want to say the name. I remember, the giveaway program called CETA where I was given a chance to get my GED. During this time I was already working for the Lord. I'm going to tell you a story. God's army is not one who shows off. I worked at the headquarters of this place long enough for God to show me how dishonest these people were. I was a keypunch operator. I didn't know how to type, but I knew how to read. People would donate items to the poor. The officers of the army would split the good things. I remember one day, a big donation came – they put it in the cafeteria. The loudspeaker came on, and the top officer went in and picked out what they wanted. Afterward, the employee's went in and got what they wanted then the poor had the leftovers. The poor got poorer, and the rich got richer.

Let me tell you about the kettles that they put out every Christmas. Let me tell you how they got paid. Let me tell you they had no bills. They live off of donations for the poor; they didn't get salaries, and they got allowances. The donation paid all their bills. I worked in the finance dept. These crooks rob Georgia citizen's blind. They took donations and paid their bills. The Georgia Bureau of investigation must move immediately is what I was thinking. The devil comes to kill, steal, and destroy. I felt I was in the right place. It wasn't nothing different to me. It was going on as if it was in the hood. You have high sadity shoplifters and hood shoplifters. We call some burglars, white collar crimes, robbers and thieves. Some appear low class but more are high class criminals. If you notice all the wire transfers, selling fake insurance policies, and the list goes on. Some are called criminals while others live in their big fat penthouses, driving fancy cars, traveling the world and living large off other people's merchandise they have stolen. I ran into hard times again, and I went back to my shoplifting. My shoplifting career took off along with the drug cartel. After looking back, I can remember lots of people that were in the drug business would get arrested after I left from selling them my merchandise. Soon afterwards they were busted. I always felt they were following me and using my trail to catch higher criminals in the drug cartel.

I went out and stole a lot of merchandise. I saw many stores that were very evil, with there was a retail of demons that soon closed down. I remember Home Improvement company, and my husband came in and jumped on me, and, but fired me because my husband beat me up in the store. This company didn't call the police and try to get me some help they just fired me on the spot. This is ridiculous. I used to go to work and work long hours. Is this justice? As soon as you try and do the right thing you just can't get ahead. Everywhere I turned the enemy was on my back; but, after all, I was sleeping with the enemy. Lord when is my life going to come?

Heaven & Hell On Candler Rd

Chapter 12

These are some horrible things I went through, and I will never forget. I came home one morning after giving birth to my precious little girl. I heard someone knocking on my door. Knock, Knock, I looked through the peephole, and it was my neighbor. She looked surprised when I answered, and then asked me, "When did you have the baby?" She just stared like she was amazed and looked down at my belly. She let me know a lady spent the night at my house last night. She must have been babysitting because she just left early this morning. I looked, and wondered why would a woman spend the night at my house while I am in the hospital, and my husband is at home? And I asked, what lady? My heart dropped because this woman was just like a sister to me. So my husband came home, and I was packing up my babies stuff. I was hurt, angry and upset. "I told him, I am done!" And, he pulled out his pistol and shot it towards me. He pulled the trigger, and the baby was in my arms, but the chamber would not release the bullet. I know there must have been angels watching over me. So, he hit me over the head with the pistol, and the bullet shot me in the back of my neck. I begin to bleed. I had a flesh wound. The angels encamped around me. The police came, and I was afraid. Someone must have heard the commotion, and I lied. I was already in the justice system, and I looked around. I was in trouble or going to jail. I knew if I would have told them the truth the police would have arrested him, and he probably would not have gotten off due to his previous charges. I didn't want my name listed on this because I too probably would have gotten in trouble. At least, this is how I thought. My history with the police is not good. And, in Georgia, when they come out on the scene they want everyone's ID. Besides, with my record things just didn't look good. Now, this reminds me of my mother's footsteps. I am in love with a man that shot me in the back of my neck and thank God the results wasn't like my mom. God wasn't finished with me. I went to the hospital, and they released me. I went back home because I didn't have anywhere to go, and I didn't tell anyone because they thought it was a drive by. Afterward, we made up once again. I thought things was going to get better after he apologized. As time went on, I thought we were getting along. So, I planned a party for him getting things prepared. I was so happy. At the party, he started calling me all sorts of curse words. He was trying to show out in front of everyone. I had promised him the next time he called me out of my name I was going to leave him. I was fed up once and for all. I started taking the pictures off the wall and packing my things. He was just a fussing and cussing. Something told me to look up and there he was with a pot of boiling water. I turned my face, and he threw it on me, but it missed my face. The hot water went down my back and legs. I ran and called the police, and they sent the fire department because they thought I said, "I was on fire." Yes, the fire was on because this was the end of our relationship. This was when he got a floater to the state of Ohio, and I eventually went to prison for stealing because I was trying to keep a roof over my children's head.

THE VOICE

Chapter 13

Message to Justice Jones from God

10/27/2015

On Tuesday morning, the Lord came to me, and said again, "Before I formed you, in your mother's womb, I knew you. I knew what you were going to do every day of your life from 07/05/1955, until every lasting day of your journey here on earth. I knew you." Thus said the Lord, "I sanctified you, and I ordained a *prophet* into this world at that tender age. I am your Master, now, then, and evermore. I have commissioned you to be a sent one to let the spirit of God speak out of your mouthpiece. I have commissioned your hands to write what I tell you to write. I've ordered your feet, to move where the Spirit of God to be like Jesus in your heart; to love, to share, and be obedient to his every word. I am the Lord, of Abraham, Jacob, and Isaiah. For you shall be a tremendous help to all whom I send to you. You do not have to be afraid of faces, for I am with you to deliver you from distractions says the Lord."

Something came over me. Then, I started thinking. The Lord will put forth his hands and touch my mouth? Behold, I will put my words, my names and accusations of anyone that I speak to or about Justice on hold. They will have no control over the contents of this story. I have only been where He sent me on the very day that I arrived in metro Atlanta. I have ordered her steps. I am the JUDGE in every courtroom that Justice Jones has been sentenced in. I had her in the places and the seasons that I wanted her in. Let no one think because he or she is in control because they're not. This book will go all over the U. S. of America, and many more nations. God have given the power to build, and to plant seeds, where they will grow. He is ready to perform His words.

Out of the North, I sent Ms. Justice Jones to the South in the year of 1979, to be about His business, Jesus Christ. I will utter my judgment against all of that, and all of them concerning their wickedness because they have forsaken me. They have also locked up my children for things that they know not.

They've removed my Ten Commandments from their courts and most government buildings. They worship the works of their hands; therefore, you as a person must prepare yourself to arise. Justice will only speak to the individuals that I command you to. Justice do not be dismayed and stay focused. Behold, I have chosen you to deliver this story of your life. It was the will of God. The great I AM. Also, the steps of a good man are ordered by the Lord, and all steps may not appear as people would want, but it's me that ordered. If there is no bad, then there can never be good. Justice, they will try to fight against you, but they will not prevail. They will do everything that God tells them to do.

"Justice, I am with you," said the Lord. "I remember you through all of your youth. I love your betrothal, when you went after me in the wilderness, in the land that I sent you. I will send disaster to all who offend you. You are my messenger. They have followed idols and have become idolaters. Never once did they say, "Where is the Lord?" He brought them out of Egypt and sat them on the bench of judgment to judge my children for their crimes.

I, Justice Jones, heard the voice of the LORD clear. If you look at the court systems today, they are all disastrous compared to many years ago. Our systems are piling up with criminals, and they are building bigger courts, and jails to contain the people. Yes, the system is blind to justice because they took the 10 Commandments out of the courtroom. The boundaries no longer exist.

I am God, who brought you into a free country to eat its fruit, and goodness, but when you entered, you defiled my land. Also, made my heritage an abomination. The law enforcement, judges, and court officials, did not ask. "Where is the Lord?" Some who handled the law did not know me. The judges transgressed against me. Thus said the Lord, The Great I am who lives and never dies, who's given Justice Jones this commission. No one can say that they are innocent before God, for he knows all. He knew her every move before she was born.

See, most of those judges don't even know the LORD or are they saved? So many enter those courts depending on the authority, and their future is in the hands of the judges. Yes, many people are guilty. Some first-time offenders and others are just innocent but sentenced. No one knows what to expect going in, yet to be convicted as they are tried. You are either guilty or not! After hearing The Lord continually speak to me, this is how He will reveal secrets of our judicial court systems to the world.

Yes, the Lord our God is angry, but you still will say that I have sinned. So, therefore, indeed, I sent out letters in 2000 and the year right after. I also sent letters in 2015 by the order of the Lord, yet you have not changed your ways, and you should be ashamed. After my time being incarcerated the Lord gave me the courage to write those letters to the justice system. I realize that I am one person being prosecuted by the justice system. The Great I am is going forth to reject them all, and they will no longer prosper. I told you all of the warnings inside those letters.

Some of the Judges truly don't have a relationship with the LORD. Also, a lot of them have not lived the life many are naturally born in such as high crime communities, poverty, and negative environments. I know some have come from terrible situations and proved themselves, but many have never tasted the dark side of life raised in dire conditions. I didn't just wake up and say I want to shoplift; and, I want to be a criminal because my wish was to join the military. Just like many murders that are on death row, and didn't wake up one morning to go murder someone. I had dreams and inspirational thoughts that I wanted, but I feel like we're led by spirits and powers that drive us in the opposite direction of our focus.

Everything plays a role in our lives from people, places, environments and things. I know I made a lot of choices, and many don't appear to be good. I don't want anyone feeling sorry for me. Yes, I committed many crimes, and I am still paying the price. As you have read my story, now you will have a better understanding how a criminal mind works.

Somethings we don't have control over once you enter into the judicial system. See; then I was in a place in my mind where I didn't know the Lord and didn't love Him. I was about 14 years old; He was so far away from me. There are a lot of people that are bitter with the Lord because of things that happened in their life just like I was. Later on, you will understand it more. I thought that my life was doomed, and God was not there for my family or me. There are many things I longed for and cried out to God before the tragic situation happened, but my prayers weren't answered. I was angry with God, why me, Lord, why me?

Letters to the Judges

Chapter 14

I want everyone to know that I sent these letters to the Judges and received no response. I did not want to list each judge separately and protect the privacy. Some Judges are good, and some are bad just like the criminals. In this world regardless of who you are there are some good, and bad people in every walk of life. Some of these judges are unfair and dishonest. I believe my story will help free a lot of individual minds that have been through the criminal system one way or another. Thinking that their lives are over and they've no chance to better themselves. Life struggles will lead many down many different paths of life, and many crimes are committed by people trying to survive, living through desperate times and feeling lost in this world. Most people know once you get a criminal record you cannot get a job because of your criminal history, and this is another mark that holds people down. I want people to understand that everyone who commits a crime is not always a criminal, but the system stereotypes people. I may seem to be nobody to many, but I am somebody to the ones that love me. I am human just like all these people that are in and out of jail, and prison systems. So many are passing judgment on people, and others get the wrong concept of characters.

I am sure that some of you are reading this book have been through what I have dealt with in the court system or knows of someone that has. One day, the Holy Spirit, moved on me and told me to write these letters. I am going to give you some examples:

Example 1:

Me and this white girl was in the Georgia area, and she took a blackberry phone and walked out the door. The store clerk wrote down my tag number and issued a warrant for my arrest and sent me to jail. It was the white lady that stole the phone, but they arrested me. I know they had cameras up in the store, but I was charged with Theft by Shoplifting. This was unjust. I had to make the bond, and I wouldn't admit to stealing the phone because it wasn't me because of my background they picked me up for a crime I didn't commit, but it's on my record.

Example 2:

I noticed on my criminal background

record they have recorded many social security numbers. I have never given my social security number going to jail, but I do know for every inmate there is money being received for each day they are incarcerated. I have names, social security numbers and numerous different dates of birth are false just as my entire criminal background record is incorrect. Um... makes you wonder who's the real criminal?

Example 3:

I want my readers to get a glimpse of my four confinements. Now, that means I would have been incarcerated in prison or a half—way house for four years straight, and that never happened, but it's on my record.

Example 4:

Now, they paint you like a career criminal and give you high fines to pay and they know you don't have any money. So, this causes you to do something wrong again. The probation fees are extremely ridiculous, and if you don't pay then, you have to go back to jail adding more to your criminal record. The system makes it more complicated to get on the right track, and everyone does not have a family with a lot of money. Nevertheless, a family with a good support system. I felt many days I was doomed because every time I tried to do right thing something else pushed me back down.

Example 5:

My background makes it looks like I am a bad person. This went on for ten years straight going back and forth; they think people don't change, but I went through this for a lifetime. Now, how can one change if the system keeps holding you back and creates criminals? So they give you these outrageous fines. It makes it difficult, to pay them. I also tried to get a place to stay plenty of times, but the apartment complex said, "I cannot let you move here with this record." So it caused even more stress to have to deal with because the items on my record are duplicated about 2 to 4 times. It stretched out your police record to make you appear three times worst. Nevertheless, the apartment people didn't know that.

Example 6:

Probation is an extended prison sentence, they monitor you, and give you high fines. It makes getting a job harder, they don't have the money, and it makes it difficult to pay your fine. A lot of people end up going back to jail because they don't have the money. See, the jail system gets money per inmate, and it's a business, not a rehab. If the state has no criminals, there would be no judges, DA's, sheriffs, police department, and attorneys, etc. and none of them would have careers. So, even criminals have a purpose. Now, don't get me wrong when a person commits a crime they should pay or do the time.

Example 7:

I have not been to prison in 20 years, and I have changed my ways.

These are just a few examples of why I wrote these letters to the Judges, and I had to experience all these situations just to write this book. God used many people for different causes. We all have different paths of life. No matter who you are everyone is going to be judged. Now, Justice Jones is just a messenger. So, if you have crime in your heart just stop because you don't want to live a life on the offensive because soon as you try and straighten out your life even more bad things will arise.

Another Letter I Sent, but No Response

From: Lady Justice

Saints in God's army

I, Diane Patterson, was sentenced by you in 1998 for shoplifting. I reviewed my case, court records when you sentenced me you said, "Ms. Patterson go down there and do your time, come back God has some work." Then you stopped and said I can't talk like that but, I got the message. There is a statue in the courtroom called Blind Justice. I am Justice Jones a voice behind the judges in every courtroom. I had a blind on me when I approached Atlanta. If you don't remember; I came in a storm in 1979. God rains down the ice all over the metro. It was me who brought the ice, the vicious blizzard. I came from the center of the world, Warren Ohio, to do God's will in my life. I know that you are a child of God, and you are waiting for this message. Now, remember, your city and the county is very corrupt, and it's time to bring justice. The blinds have been removed from the blind justice statue, just like from the Ten Commandments was withdrawn from the courthouse.

I was in the Georgia department of corrections off and on at numerous facilities. As an inmate, I was able to speculate and pinpoint different flaws and corruptions; not just by the prisoners, but also the staff. I am not trying to make excuses for what I did when I lived in a different mindset and made excuses for my life, but it makes a huge difference how your life is. Some things traumatized me even until this day I had to learn to live and do better. Not all my choices were good, and many were wrong. But if I would not have experienced being raped, my mother being murdered at a young age, experiencing drugs, sex and violence most of my life then perhaps I would not have a story. I am not trying to justify my acts, but I still know I had to live this mortal life. So someone be can granted a new life.

The Wide Road On Ember Drive

Chapter 15

I used to live with different people trying to save money. I refused to live with anyone else. I grew tired, I was homeless, and some angels of mine let me stay with them for three weeks then the Lord sent me to Ember Drive. I saw these apartments down the street this place was ragged, trashy but I found out they were cheap, and I needed a roof over my head. I did not want to be in the trap where the drugs were because I was clean. But, I need a place. So I inquired about one bedroom, and I found out I can afford this. I needed something immediately. I got tired of living from place to place and staying with other people. It was a time I get it together and get back on my feet. After I had applied for the apartment, I got it. I didn't care what it looked like just as long as it was mine. I was so excited something is finally going right for me.

As I walked into the apartment, it smelled like the pits of hell. It had a stinky smell, I cleaned and deodorized. The apartment manager didn't tell me someone was murdered in it. I couldn't believe it I am living in an apartment someone died in. I heard it was a horrible death. Everywhere I looked it was crime, drugs, prostitution, theft and killing. I got to find a way to reach these people because too many are dying at such a young age. Poverty has a way of taking a toll on everyone.

I was laying on my bed The Holy Spirit spoke to me. He said, "Tell all my people God got a plan for us." We are the ones that will lead the people out of the hood, from drugs and prostitution. Come from among them, and tell them God has healed this land." We will be the one to lead them out of their dope traps. You see, dope traps are houses that help people smoke dope in, get introduced to the devils trap. A place where people get so caught up, and lured in for years. A place that misleads the lost guide the hopeless, and disfigure the dreams of healthy families. It is the entrance to hell on earth. The difference between hell on land, and eternal hell here you have the opportunity to come out. I thank God I made it out before eternal hell took place because that one there is no turning around ever. This is Satan's permanent address, and he want as much company as he can get. It doesn't matter your background, education, nationality, or degrees. He just intends to take as many people down with him as he could. His primary objective is sorcery. After I realized this, I just shook my head. That Joker has so many fooled.

Chapter 16

Sorcery

I have seen so many people get caught up in these trap houses. A place where people are introduced to drugs, and buy them. So many come in one way and exit another. The hell that they are getting ready to go through only God knows, I know. I got to stop it some way. This is one door you don't ever want to open. Rock cocaine! You must understand everything Jesus created Satan duplicated. Jesus is the ROCK, and Satan duplicated His rock. The rock Satan duplicated is full of evil and fear, but Jesus rock is power, love and of a sound mind. The devil's rock is a trick from the devil. The more a person uses it, the more they want it. It makes many stay away from their kids, and family for weeks at a time. Just like Jesus the more you get Him, the more you are going to want Him. See, how the devil tried to duplicate everything Jesus does because he wants to kill, steal and destroy our minds.

Merriam Dictionary

Sorcery:

1) the use of power gained from the assistance or control of evil spirits especially for divining: necromancy

2) Magic

the use of magic which is witchcraft

Satan is the author of confusion using sorcery and witchcraft. Drugs have a firm hold which causes addition to the mind. This is the same effect drugs have on people, they are strong; but, take control of one's mind and then ruin their life. I used to see people go in, and out of these drug houses like a revolving door just to get high. If they weren't going in and out of these doors, it was the justice system. Lower class, high class, professional and unprofessional people are addicted too. I used to see just as many professional people getting high more than you know. One thing leads to another. So many women and girls would sell their bodies to these professional men with wedding bands on and would pay these girls for their services. Prostituting for pennies on a dollar. These girls dressed like tramps. Some of them have not seen their children in weeks because they left them with their parents, grandparents, neighbor or strangers. All they can think about is getting high. The drugs have possessed their minds.

One day I had an accident on Ember Drive, and the officer knew the guy that caused the wreck but wrote me a ticket. This guy was under the influence of drugs and alcohol when I went to court. God threw the tickets out. I have seen doctors, lawyers, law enforcement and every profession hitting the rock, doing drugs or snorting cocaine. If the devil can control your mind he can control your destiny that is why I say the rock is the mark of the beast.

I saw this one person I did not want to see them go down that road. It is this new drug called Molly they say, "Molly." I say, "Holy," once again Satan is trying to duplicate Jesus. Molly is a pill with Meth in it. It is a target for the hood. It's cheap and not as expensive as Meth. Most poor people cannot afford cocaine which is imitated as rock and Molly imitated as Meth. Molly makes you mad, angry and evil. I saw this person walk in a trap house and buy one. It hurt me to my heart. I watched this person almost lose everything that God had in store for him. So I went to Fresh Wind Christian Church, and I went to the Saints. I cried my heart out to them for people that used that drug, and together we prayed then I noticed a change had taken place. Isn't this something. I was watching the news and found out the President was coming to Georgia. So I made plans to hear his speech. I wanted to get my book in his hands. On March 29, 2016, I saw President Barack Obama downtown Atlanta getting off the plane. I was amazed he came all the way here to address drugs. It touched my heart. He was talking about the same thing I was speaking of in my book. He was addressing the drug situation in ways to help those that are in need of drug rehabilitation, and people that are affected by drugs. As he was speaking, I was stunned because I was in the last chapter of my books, and he was hitting on this topic. We were thinking on the same path and on one accord.

Heroin is the most addictive drug that I know and has caused so many to commit suicide, and overdose in my eye-sight for all I have experienced. Satan sends out pharmaceutical drugs to kill, steal and destroy peoples' lives when they cannot get prescription medicine they go to street drugs. Each generation has had some form of the drug to destroy the minds of them and their family members, loves ones, and to destroy their lives. Satan's primary focus is to steal the family joy, separate the loved ones and destroy the minds of God's people. Satan is doing an excellent job. These drugs caused people to steal, kill and destroy such as these evil spirits.

Alcohol is the most acceptable drug, but many abuse it too. Look at the prison system, jails, graveyards, mental hospitals, and people going against one another. These drugs are inducing individuals with an evil that causes control of the mind which is witchcraft from the devil. The evil spirit is strong, mighty and controlling then you wonder why we have drive by killings, serious suicide attempts, murdering spirits lingering everywhere, and in Georgia our alcohol stores say spirits. Everybody's investing in all the spirits and they are coming in legions to take over.

After God had delivered me out of the wilderness back into His Kingdom, my rock changed. My rock changed because He is my Rock. I know that is the only way people are going to get clean. Their first steps to coming clean and staying clean is Jesus. I owe God for what He has done for me. I want to tell you what God has done for me. He took me out of the pits of hell here on earth. No one can tell me hell is not here on earth and nobody can tell me hell don't exist in the land. One thing I realized about the addicts is they will go to work and make money for this dope. I know it comes from the professional people bringing all this crap into the ghettos. The only way you are going to clean the drugs up is that you have to get to the root of the source and start at the top. So many try, and speak badly against the addicts, but it's the business professional and rich people that bring it in. Once again, the rich are getting richer, and the poorer are getting poorer.

Acknowledgment

My Attorney Mike Maloof

My Bails Bondsman Free At Last Bail Bonds Company
Cathy Joyce

Fresh Wind Christian Church

My Pastor Steven D. Byrd Sr. Pastor

My Friend Parice C. Parker

Anthony Coleman

Ethel C. Beaver

Mary Lemons

John & Joanne Richardson

Valdeoso & Regina Patterson

Strange, but UNIQUE!

Paul & Mary Andrews

Arlene & Chiquita Bills

Vanessa Jones

Patrica Monds & Son

Irene Hugely & Family

Mr Harris & Cheryl S. Hall

Thomas Jackson

Brenda Millines

Thomas Millines

Anthony Heard

Virginia B. Sinkfield

Eula Seals

Strange, but UNIQUE!

Gwendolyn Brock

Cutting Edge – Deedria Williams

James Venable & Mother

Jerry & Mary Patterson

Maxine Franklin

Lowell Moses

Floyd & Avon Jacobs

Albert & Carrie Jones

Carolyn Jones

Felicia Jones

Theresa Jones

Kimberly Jones

Jake Jones

Sherry Gains

Iris McKay

www.PeoplesTV.com– Reverend Ben

Susie Cunningham

To all My Loving Aunts, Uncles, Cousins, Friends and all my God children. To all of my true, and loving supporters that was a true inspiration to my life and children's lives.

I want to name everyone but it's impossible. My heart says thanks to everyone who loved me on this journey.

Diane Patterson is a native of Warren Ohio, and currently resides in the Georgia area. God has granted her two beautiful daughters and four fabulous grandchildren. She is a very proud mother and grandmother.

She is a graduate of Warren Western Reserve High School and received her cosmetologist license in 1979 from Lewis Weinberger in Hill Beauty School in Warren Ohio.

Diane Patterson went to Georgia Perimeter College in Georgia as a key punch operator. She also received her Barber's License and Cosmetology Instructor License from the Hair Schools, LLC. On Candler Road in Decatur, Georgia. Mrs. Diane B. Patterson also received her Phlebotomy License from the VA Hospital in Decatur, Georgia.

To all the host of people who made it possible, and that took care of my children during my absence while on this tedious journey. It was a course of life I was commissioned for the contents of this book, the introduction of more, to find my purpose in life, and to be the voice for others living with terrible traumatic life experiences. 24 Felonies & 24 Alias' it's strange but unique.

Diane Beaver Patterson

aka Justice Jones

Contact Information for Diane B. Patterson

aka Justice Jones

P. O. Box 360146 Decatur, Georgia, 30034

Email: justicejones2016@yahoo.com

To place book orders, book signing, interviews and to request Justice Jones for motivational speaking engagements please log on here

Website: www.justicejones.org

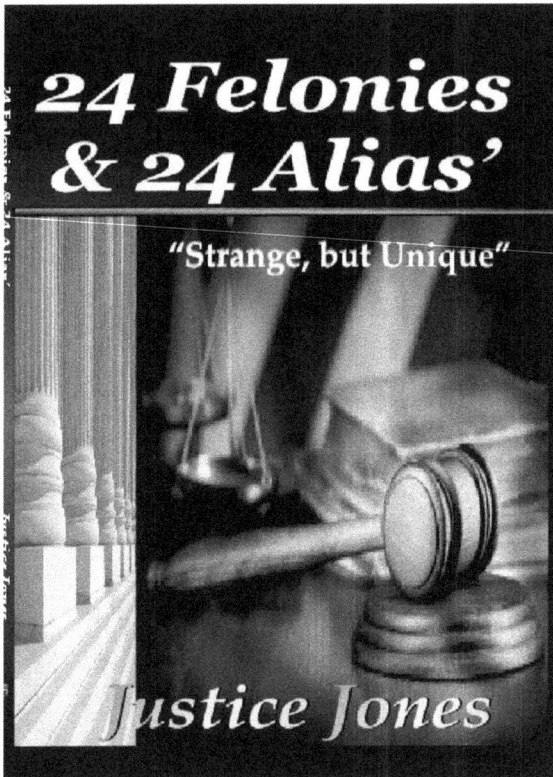

Order Here & Where Ever Books Are Sold

Www.justicejones.org

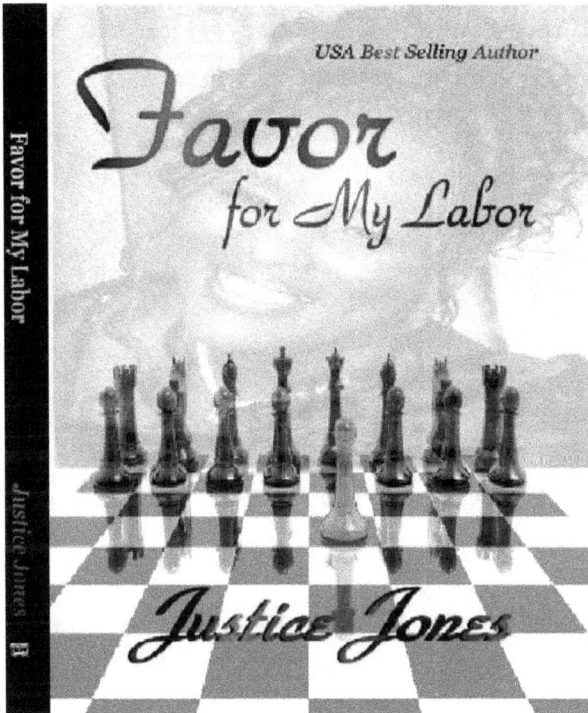

Favor for My Labor

Law / Conflict of Laws

I was here during the era of The Missing & Murdered Children of Atlanta. There were no cell phones, and video cameras to record the evil activities, but I come to tell you anything you do in the dark will come to the light. Can't you see God is revealing it each, and every day? To do something about this, we must Get to the root of it, and the root must be uprooted. So therefore, I am going to do my part by Unlocking the Secrets that I have experience in the Blind Criminals Justice Systems because it was designed to make people look like career criminals. Get in line for Favor for My Labor...$19.95

Order Here & Where Ever Books Are Sold

Www.justicejones.org

Fountain of Life Publishers House

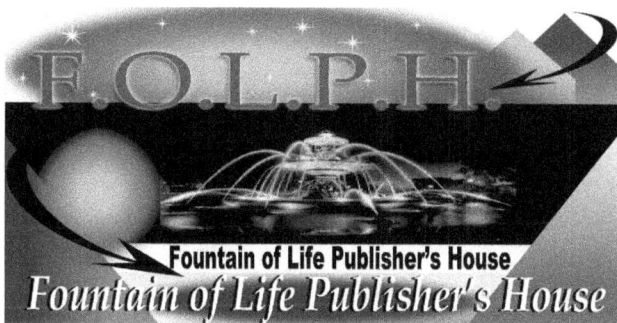

P. O. Box 922612, Norcross, GA 30010
Phone: 404.936.3989

For book orders or wholesale distribution
Website: www.pariceparker.biz

Strange, but UNIQUE!